CHILD-CENTRED CO-PARENTING

Tracey Duff and Daniella Rigon

with
Bev Aisbett

CHILD-CENTRED CO-PARENTING

First published in Australia 2018
by CoParenting Crew
Copyright ©Tracey Duff and Daniella Rigon 2017

Copyright illustrations and illustrated format
©Bev Aisbett 2017
www.bevaisbettartofanxiety.com

ABN 89953700775

ISBN 978-0-9875301-2-7

This book is copyright.
Apart from the uses of personal study,
research, criticism or review, no part may be
reproduced without written permission by
the copyright holders.

Enquiries should be addressed to:

PO BOX 122
Hunters Hill 2110

Website www.coparentingcrew.com

Facebook – https://www.facebook.com/CoParentingCrew/

Twitter - https://twitter.com/CoParentingCrew

YouTube - https://www.youtube.com/user/CoParentingCrew

Cover illustration by Bev Aisbett

*For Josh, who allows us to use his story
so that other children may benefit.*

DISCLAIMER

This book is based on the strategies we used in our blended family. We are not doctors, lawyers or professional counsellors. We are simply a family that has chosen to share our story. This book is not intended to replace or dispute professional advice and has been shared to illustrate the unique way in which we chose to deal with our family situation. We strongly encourage everyone in a similar situation to seek professional advice before making decisions for your family or personal situation.

FOREWORD

When our extremely volatile marriage came to an end, there were many decisions that needed to be made. The most important of these was how we could minimize the effect that our divorce had on our son Josh. We understood the value that both parents would add to his life so tried to focus on a way to make this possible for him.

Initially, for both of us, it was almost unbearable to be apart from our son, particularly when he was sick or upset about something. Over time, we learnt to cope with our new "normal" and instead focused on what we could control.

Throughout our journey and our many challenges we learnt fundamental skills and strategies that enabled us to co-parent successfully. Over time we met many other families who seemed to be struggling with the same issues that we had once experienced. Most were very surprised that we were able to not only co-parent our son, but also do this peacefully. We knew that although we weren't trained professionals in divorce or parenting, our experiences had given a valuable insight into what could be helpful to other families.

Child-Centred Co-Parenting is a collaboration by my son's stepmother Daniella and myself. As a teacher, Daniella has been exposed to the negative impact that divorce can have on children and was keen to help educate families about the benefits of placing children's needs first.

Our hope is that this book will enable families to move past their hurts in order to be able to also co-parent successfully, not only for the sake of their children, but for themselves as well.

CONTENTS

	Our Blended Family	1
CHAPTER 1	D.I.V.O.R.C.E	10
CHAPTER 2	The Reality Check	16
CHAPTER 3	Getting the Right Help	29
CHAPTER 4	The "F" Word	37
CHAPTER 5	Moving On	49
CHAPTER 6	Why Share Custody?	54
CHAPTER 7	Joint Custody	61
CHAPTER 8	What If My Ex Won't Co-Parent?	70
CHAPTER 9	Formulating a Parenting Plan	76
CHAPTER 10	Essential Ingredients in Sharing Custody	86
CHAPTER 11	Child Support - Show Me the Money	99
CHAPTER 12	Talking About Your Ex	105
CHAPTER 13	Parental Alienation	109
CHAPTER 14	Letting Go of Control	117
CHAPTER 15	Dating For Single Parents	124
	The Final Word	131

Our Blended Family

Hi, I'm TRACEY! DAVE and I were once MARRIED.

I'm DAVE and together TRACEY and I had our son, JOSH.

I'm SCOTT, TRACEY'S second husband...

...and I'm DANIELLA, DAVE'S second wife.

And we are Josh's STEP-PARENTS.

We've come together to share with you our story of CO-OPERATIVE CO-PARENTING...

...and to let you know that not only is it POSSIBLE to achieve this...

...it's VITALLY IMPORTANT that you find a way to do so...

...not only for your OWN peace of mind...

... but especially for your CHILDREN'S sake!

We know first-hand that it's NOT EASY...

...but it IS doable and we're here to show you how WE did it...

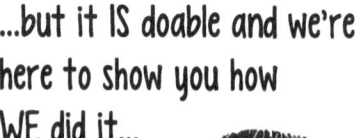

...so that hopefully, YOU TOO, can be harmoniously blended...

...into two households that work together to create SECURE and SUPPORTIVE HOMES...

...and cooperate as a TEAM, instead of being COMPETITORS...

...REGARDLESS of any previous (or current) DIFFERENCES!

And of COURSE there will be differences!

If there weren't you wouldn't be DIVORCED in the first place...

...and some of those will remain CHALLENGING!

Whilst the BRADY BUNCH depicts an IDEALISED DREAM...

...REALITY is an entirely DIFFERENT matter!

But here is the ESSENTIAL POINT...

You are the ADULTS...

...and the child is just a CHILD...

And as ADULTS, we have RESPONSIBILITIES – and RIGHTS – that need to be NEGOTIATED and EXPLORED for successful CO-PARENTING...

...and the BEST interests of the CHILD!

The fact that you may now feel hostile towards each other is not the child's FAULT, nor his/her PROBLEM to fix.

This is an ADULT concern.

He or she still needs what EVERY child needs –

LOVE

SECURITY

and SAFETY

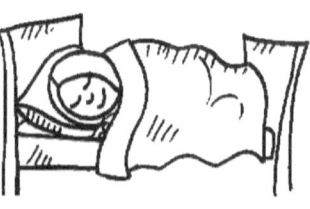

As ADULTS, that is what you need to focus on providing – REGARDLESS of your own hurt at this time.

So hopefully you're ready to join us on our journey from SEPARATION...

...to CO-OPERATION!

And last, but not LEAST, here is the person at the CENTRE of this book...

...this is JOSH – who has grown into a well-balanced young man who knows he is LOVED by ALL of his parents.

CHAPTER 1

D.I.V.O.R.C.E

Let's face it, no-one goes into MARRIAGE with a plan to DIVORCE...

And here are your divorce papers — JUST IN CASE!

...but, for whatever reason, that's where you've ENDED UP.

Separation and divorce can be a time of great EMOTIONAL UPHEAVAL — in fact, it can be one of the most painful experiences you'll ever go through — especially if there are CHILDREN involved.

We will explore how to deal with these powerful emotions in the coming chapter but the bottom line is that it is NORMAL to go through them at this time!

You are experiencing significant LOSS and UPHEAVAL so EXPECT to feel STRONG EMOTIONS.

But remember that this early phase is the WORST OF IT. In time, these feelings will EASE.

A common emotion in this early stage is BLAME.

You know, it really was all HER fault!

Whilst it may be tempting to put all the BLAME onto your EX for the demise of your relationship; in reality it takes TWO people to MAKE or BREAK it.

For one person to take all the BLAME, the other person must not have been involved at ALL, which is simply not POSSIBLE – unless...

Ok I guess it must be all MY fault!

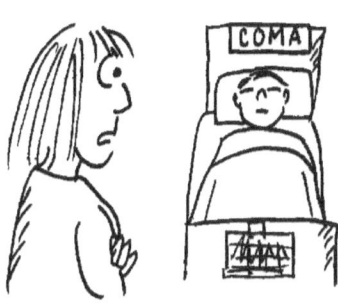

You need to acknowledge that EACH of you has CONTRIBUTED to the breakdown of your relationship...

But he was a BULLY!

...and the role that each partner plays may not necessarily constitute a CLEARCUT 50/50 split of the BLAME!

While one party may SEEM to be more RESPONSIBLE for damaging the relationship, how the other party RESPONDS is also a contributing factor.

Every situation is DIFFERENT and when you're deep in HURT, it is likely that you will see yourself as the wounded party and you may have every reason to believe this to be true.

But no matter how EXTREME your break-up was for the two of you, there needs to be one PRIMARY CONCERN –**TO MINIMISE THE IMPACT OF YOUR SEPARATION ON YOUR CHILDREN.**

Putting your OWN FEELINGS ASIDE whilst attending to your child's feelings can help to ease the effect that your separation has on him or her.

Does it really matter who was RIGHT or WRONG if your child is SUFFERING because of your ANGER at EACH OTHER?

Remember — your child loves *BOTH* of YOU!

The common trap for couples going through separation and divorce is to think in terms of RIGHT or WRONG; WINNERS and LOSERS...

...but when there is a 'war' going on, there are only CASUALTIES – YOU, YOUR EX and especially YOUR CHILDREN! NOBODY WINS THIS WAR!

But we discovered a way where EVERYONE can win and we're going to share that with you now...

... but first up we need to get a REALITY CHECK out of the way!

CHAPTER 2

The Reality Check

As tough as it is, you need to face the fact that no matter what you do, your separation is going to emotionally affect your child in SOME way.

The impact may be:

WITNESSING PARENTS' EMOTIONAL DISTRESS

REDUCED OR LIMITED CONTACT WITH PARENT/S

CHANGES TO LIVING ARRANGEMENTS

MORE TIME IN TRANSIT

CHANGES TO SOCIAL CONTACTS

FEELINGS OF INSECURITY

THE CHILD'S OWN EMOTIONAL RESPONSE TO THE BREAK-UP

There will be many things to consider when you split from your partner but the three things that require your IMMEDIATE ATTENTION are:

1. YOUR OWN EMOTIONAL WELLBEING

The ending of a relationship – especially when CHILDREN are involved – can give rise to an overwhelming range of EMOTIONS such as:

SADNESS	**GUILT**
ANXIETY	**NUMBNESS**
CONFUSION	**AND** **DESPAIR**

You may also experience FEARS around:

- **BEING ALONE WITHOUT YOUR PARTNER**
- **YOUR PARTNER BEING WITH SOMEONE ELSE**
- **WHAT THE FUTURE WILL BRING**
- **LOSING MUTUAL FRIENDS**
- **WHERE YOU WILL LIVE**
- **YOUR FINANCES**
- **CHANGES TO YOUR LIFESTYLE**
- **WHAT FAMILY AND FRIENDS WILL THINK**
- **HOW YOUR CHILDREN WILL COPE**
- **HOW YOU'LL MANAGE ON YOUR OWN**

How am I going to COPE?

Whilst we emphasise that the CHILD'S NEEDS are paramount, looking after yourself at this time is CRUCIAL so that you are EQUIPPED to look after your child's needs.

You are in a much better position to look after your children and cope with the challenges you need to work through if you firstly attend to your OWN WELLBEING.

Think of self-care as being like the SAFETY INSTRUCTIONS (that everyone ignores) on aeroplanes:

Parents, please place YOUR oxygen mask on first before attending to your CHILD'S mask!

You need to be in the BEST SHAPE you can be to help your child through this difficult time, so:

LOOK AFTER YOU!

2. YOUR CHILDREN'S WELLBEING

Although you are navigating your way through some incomprehensible feelings at the moment, no matter how difficult it may seem, you need to formulate a plan for the INTERIM CUSTODY of your children.

An INTERIM CUSTODY ARRANGEMENT is a short-term plan that is put into place to determine:

- WHERE THE CHILD/CHILDREN WILL LIVE
- WHO WILL BE RESPONSIBLE FOR THEIR DAY TO DAY CARE IN THE SHORT-TERM

This is put in place until a PERMANENT ARRANGEMENT is agreed to by both parents or set out by either the courts or mediation.

THE NEEDS OF CHILDREN MAY DIFFER AND THEIR WELLBEING SHOULD BE THE MOST IMPORTANT FACTOR.

Assuming there is no ABUSE or NEGLECT and that both parents are FIT, WILLING and ABLE, it is important that children have access to their parents EQUALLY; no matter how temporary the arrangement.

This is because regular contact with both parents provides:

- **CONSISTENCY**
- **STABILITY**
- **THE OPPORTUNITY TO CONTINUE TO DEVELOP A RELATIONSHIP WITH BOTH PARENTS**

How do we do that when we're in the middle of all these PAINFUL EMOTIONS?

We can hardly even LOOK at each other, let alone AGREE!

We viewed it THIS WAY...

...the care of Josh was SEPARATE to the END of our RELATIONSHIP!

 So why should he suffer the consequences of OUR PAIN?

Josh needed ACCESS to both of us just as he did before we split

...in fact, he needed it more than EVER at this time!

Denying your child a relationship with their other parent will not diminish YOUR pain; it will only enhance THEIR pain!

Keeping your emotions out of the custody plan will almost always produce a more positive result for the child.

We focussed on the fact that our LOVE for JOSH was MORE IMPORTANT than our ISSUES with each other.

Appointing a COUNSELLOR for your child is also essential to provide a safe space for them to work through the situation with a non-biased outsider.

We also talked OPENLY and HONESTLY with Josh and encouraged him to do the SAME.

We wanted him to know that OUR break-up wasn't HIS fault...

...and that we each
loved him
UNCONDITIONALLY!

3. YOUR FINANCES

The third item that needs your attention at this time is your FINANCES.

This is one of the most CONTROVERSIAL and COMPLEX issues that will arise from your separation.

BOTH PARTIES' FINANCIAL SITUATION WILL BE AFFECTED BY YOUR SEPARATION OR DIVORCE.

Many people may see it THIS WAY:

'He earns MORE than me, so he should PAY more'

Why should I fork out? She's going to send me BROKE!

Again, this is about putting the needs of the CHILD first.

In reality, BOTH parents need to be financially stable for the wellbeing of the child.

If one parent is left struggling in POVERTY or SQUALOR, the child will live that way when they are in that parent's care. Do you want that for them?

Sorry, kids but it's BAKED BEANS again!

Providing two loving and financially stable households benefits EVERYONE.

Making this happen may involve a lot of ADJUSTMENTS:

- **YOU MAY NOT BE ABLE TO REMAIN IN THE FAMILY HOME**
- **THERE WILL BE ADDITIONAL EXPENSES FOR THE PARTNER WHO MOVED OUT**
- **THERE MAY ALSO BE A LOSS OF INCOME WHEN TWO HOUSEHOLDS NEED TO BE FUNDED**
- **THERE MAY NEED TO BE NEW ARRANGEMENTS REGARDING WORK**

It is important that you think LONG-TERM when sorting out financial arrangements.

CHAPTER 3

Getting the Right Help

You may be wondering when this PAIN will end or when obsessive THOUGHTS such as these will STOP:

I wonder what he's DOING?

I wonder where she's GOING?

What if she's met SOMEONE ELSE?

He didn't seem to be as upset as ME!

I don't think I can BEAR this loneliness!

What if this is a TERRIBLE MISTAKE?

There is no doubt about it – going through a separation or divorce can be an extremely TRAUMATIC experience for all the members of the family.

It is absolutely vital that you set up a SUPPORT NETWORK for yourself and your children at this time.

Enlisting the help of a professional therapist can be invaluable to ensure you are MENTALLY and EMOTIONALLY in check.

The role of a therapist is to act as an impartial OBSERVER and CONFIDANTE who can offer emotional support and help you to:

- **PROCESS YOUR EMOTIONS**
- **REGAIN YOUR EQUILIBRIUM**
- **IDENTIFY YOUR STRENGTHS**
- **MODIFY YOUR WEAKNESSES**
- **STRATEGISE THE WAY FORWARD**
- **PUT IN PLACE A SELF-CARE PLAN**

There are also some simple things that you can do to help yourself feel better:

GET PLENTY OF SLEEP

EAT HEALTHY FOODS

DRINK PLENTY OF WATER

GET OUT IN THE SUNSHINE

DO SOME FORM OF EXERCISE - EVEN A SHORT WALK

TALK TO SOMEONE WHO IS SUPPORTIVE

Above all, avoid the temptation to BURY your pain in UNHELPFUL BEHAVIOURS such as:

BINGE DRINKING   SITTING UP ALL NIGHT OBSESSING

OR RETREATING ENTIRELY

Whilst this might seem to be a way to COPE in the short-term, coming back from these can make life much HARDER. Do you really want to ADD to your PROBLEMS? If you need HELP with COPING, it's important that you REACH OUT.

It is also important that you give your children the opportunity to have access to PROFESSIONAL COUNSELLING. It will help to provide:

- **WAYS TO DEAL WITH THE SITUATION**
- **COPING SKILLS THAT THEY CAN UTILISE THROUGHOUT THEIR LIVES**
- **A SAFE HAVEN TO EXPRESS THEMSELVES WITHOUT FEAR OF JUDGMENT**

You can also help your children by:

- **HAVING THEM FOLLOW YOUR SELF-CARE PLAN**
- **OPEN LINES OF COMMUNICATION**
- **KEEPING THE GORY DETAILS OF YOUR SEPARATION TO YOURSELF**
- **KEEPING ADULT ISSUES FOR THE ADULTS**
- **REAFFIRMING THAT THE CHILD IS LOVED BY BOTH PARENTS**
- **REAFFIRMING THAT THE CHILD IS IN NO WAY RESPONSIBLE FOR THE BREAKDOWN**
- **SPEAKING KINDLY ABOUT YOUR EX IN FRONT OF THE CHILD AND OTHERS**
- **KEEPING A CLOSE EYE ON HOW YOU BEHAVE AROUND YOUR CHILD AS YOU HAVE A HUGE INFLUENCE ON THEM**

A JOURNAL is also a great way to help your child OPEN UP about how they feel, especially if they find it difficult to express their feelings FACE to FACE.

Explain to the child that they can use the journal as a different way of 'speaking' to you and that it is meant for you to read so that you can better understand their FEELINGS. You might like to suggest TOPICS to get them started such as:

- 'I wish my parents knew…'
- 'I feel hurt when…'
- 'I feel happy when…'
- 'I don't like it when…'
- 'I like it when…'
- 'I would like more of…'
- 'I wish I/we could…'

Finally, communicate with your child's SCHOOL to let them know what is happening. Teachers spend a lot of time with your child and may be able to help or keep a close eye on BEHAVIOURAL CHANGES that might signal that your child needs extra help.

Also ask other ELDERS such as COACHES or RELATIVES to report any behavioural issues they might observe.

I've noticed my child is ACTING OUT!

It isn't uncommon for children to display some BEHAVIOURAL CHANGES after you split up, which is hardly surprising as this may be the only way they can PROCESS the feelings of LOSS, FRUSTRATION or ANGER that result from such UPHEAVAL in their lives.

Most children are not emotionally mature enough to fully understand why their parents are no longer together, so their frustration and stress may manifest in changed behaviour which may range from MILD ACTING OUT to DESTRUCTIVE BEHAVIOUR.

Whilst this is usually a PASSING PHASE, it is important that you keep an eye on SIGNIFICANT or LASTING changes.

It is also essential that you COMMUNICATE with your ex about your observations. The child may display different behaviours in front of either parent.

Especially watch for DEPRESSION or AGGRESSION and seek professional help if necessary.

CHAPTER 4

The 'F' Word

When it comes to your ex, you may have been using plenty of the other kind, but in this chapter, we're going to explore an entirely different 'F' word!

When your relationship breaks down, there is inevitably a great deal of HURT, RESENTMENT and ANGER that precedes it and the biggest challenge can be letting go of these feelings towards your ex.

But no matter how HURT or ANGRY you may feel towards your ex, the BOTTOM LINE is that NOTHING is more DAMAGING to your child as when YOU or YOUR EX put each other down in their presence.

People find many reasons to HOLD ONTO hurt.

You may indeed feel HARD DONE BY; not only by your ex but by the LEGAL PROCESS, the FINANCIAL BURDEN or the RADICAL CHANGES in your circumstances. You may feel that you are totally RIGHT and your ex is totally WRONG.

He CHEATED on me!

She LIED to me!

There may be a million reasons for you to want to SCREAM:

I was WRONGED!

But for your OWN GOOD, you need to LET THIS GO.

You cannot put your own and your children's WELLBEING in jeopardy just to prove that you were RIGHT (which may never be actually PROVEN).

CONSIDER THIS:

If you could UNDO the separation, would you really go BACK to this person?

Would you want to be with someone who no longer LOVES you?

Isn't it BETTER that you have PARTED, rather than staying together in MISERY?

Hmm...when you put it THAT way...

When it comes down to it, staying ANGRY with someone takes a HUGE toll on YOU and your CHILDREN.

You have to invest a lot of ENERGY into keeping hold of that ANGER, HURT and PAIN; energy that could be used for MOVING ON and REBUILDING your life. You are FREE to do that but not if you are TIED to WHO DID WHAT TO WHOM, which may NEVER be resolved to your satisfaction.

But if I let this go, won't she have GOTTEN AWAY WITH IT?

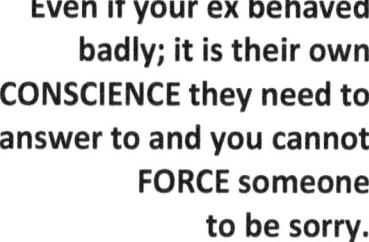

Even if your ex behaved badly; it is their own CONSCIENCE they need to answer to and you cannot FORCE someone to be sorry.

Besides, they may see it differently to you! When you are deep in HURT, you tend to see only your ex's FAILINGS and not your OWN.

But I've been so HURT— how can I move on?

There is only one way:

FORGIVENESS

FORGIVENESS MEANS:

- **UNHOOKING YOURSELF FROM THE PAIN**
- **RELEASING SELF-PITY THAT KEEPS YOU POWERLESS**
- **NO LONGER LETTING HURT DEFINE YOU**
- **ACKNOWLEDGING THAT HUMANS MAKE MISTAKES**
- **LEAVING THE PAST IN THE PAST**
- **FREEING YOURSELF TO START AGAIN**
- **NOT LETTING YOUR EX'S BEHAVIOUR CONTROL YOUR OWN WELLBEING**

The easiest way to move forward with forgiveness is to alter your MINDSET from:

SELF-CENTRED to **CHILD-CENTRED**

My ex left ME and the CHILDREN when he had his affair! 	He left our RELATIONSHIP; not our CHILDREN! 
I won't COPE without MY KIDS!	My children shouldn't MISS OUT because of how I feel! 
The courts awarded ME primary custody! 	Our children have TWO PARENTS and deserve the time and love of BOTH! 

She ALIENATED ME from my children!

Speaking badly of her only hurts MY CHILDREN more!

Remember, we're not talking about a STRANGER or DISTANT RELATIVE. This parent is someone your child LOVES as much as you. When we make one parent redundant from their lives, it hurts THEM. PERIOD!

And remember that the one who HANGS ONTO anger, is the one who is LEFT WITH IT!

FORGIVENESS is an ACT and a DECISION and it may mean that you have to do the OPPOSITE to how you feel for a while. It means being MINDFUL of what you choose to FOCUS on – HURT or HEALING.

Letting go of hurt also makes room for BETTER THINGS to come into your life, such as new INTERESTS or the chance of LOVING and BEING LOVED by someone else.

But I SUFFERED really BADLY — other people don't go through as much!

There is no way to measure one person's PAIN against another's.

PAIN is PAIN. There is no point in COMPARING or using your situation as an EXCUSE to stay STUCK.

Now that you have forgiven your ex (WELL DONE!) there is something equally or even more important for you to do...you need to:

FORGIVE YOURSELF!

Forgiving yourself helps you to:

- **FREE YOURSELF FROM PARALYSING GUILT**
- **GIVE YOURSELF PERMISSION TO BE LESS THAN PERFECT**
- **RELEASE THE NEED TO BLAME YOURSELF FOR YOUR PAIN OR THE PAIN OF YOUR CHILDREN**
- **ACKNOWLEDGE YOUR HUMANNESS AND IMPERFECTIONS**
- **LEAVE BEHIND THE PAST AND MOVE ON**

Now you've made the decision to FORGIVE and MOVE FORWARD, you need to STICK WITH IT.

But I still find it hard to keep my COOL with my ex at times!

It can be easy to BACKSLIDE and dredge up the past when emotions are high or there is a DISAGREEMENT. Again, you must remember to place your CHILD'S NEEDS above your own feelings. If you feel yourself losing CONTROL, try these STRATEGIES:

I need some TIME-OUT but I'll be BACK!

Respectfully end the conversation and pick it up again when you're feeling CALMER. It is also important that you reassure your ex that you will RESUME the conversation and not just DISAPPEAR.

STOP for a few seconds and focus on a HELPFUL MANTRA such as:

MY CHILD IS MORE IMPORTANT THAN MY ANGER

Say WE. Using 'WE' rather than 'I' feels less like an attack and invites more CO-OPERATION in solving an issue TOGETHER.

OK, how can WE work on this?

ACKNOWLEDGE the other person's EFFORTS.

I know you also want THE BEST for the kids...

HOW you say something is more important than WHAT you say.
Be MINDFUL of how you COME ACROSS. Are you inviting a PEACEFUL solution or are you on the ATTACK?

TAKE TURNS. Make an agreement that each person speaks in TURN without INTERRUPTION. That way, each feels HEARD.

FORGIVENESS also opens the way to better COMMUNICATION as you are free to deal with PRESENT ISSUES without the PAST getting in the way.

CHAPTER 5

Moving On

People separate or divorce for different reasons and no two situations will be the same.

This also applies to the rate at which either partner MOVES ON.

This can be distressing for the partner who doesn't RECOVER as quickly as the other...

How could he have MOVED ON already? Didn't I mean anything?

...and especially DIFFICULT when your ex-partner doesn't deal with the break-up in the way that you EXPECTED them to.

She's LAUGHING! How can she Be HAPPY?

Witnessing your ex moving on before you're ready to can be GUT-WRENCHING and it may be especially challenging in this phase to remember your pact of putting your CHILDREN'S needs first.

Okay, so here are a few things to CONSIDER:

- **YOU CANNOT KNOW WHAT IS IN SOMEONE ELSE'S HEART OR HEAD SO DON'T GUESS**
- **YOUR EX MAY BE FEELING THE SAME PAIN AS YOU BUT PROCESSING IT DIFFERENTLY OR AT A LATER TIME**
- **WE EACH GRIEVE AND MOVE ON IN OUR OWN TIME – THERE IS NO PRESCRIBED TIME LIMIT OR WAY TO DO IT**
- **WHAT YOUR EX IS DOING DOES NOT GOVERN YOUR WELLBEING - YOU DO**
- **THE DAY YOU SEPARATE IS THE LAST TIME YOU ARE INVOLVED WITH EACH OTHER'S PRIVATE LIVES (APART FROM THE CARE OF YOUR CHILD)**

In time, the intense feelings that you are experiencing will SUBSIDE.

You can HASTEN the process by:

RECLAIMING YOUR SPACE

I've always wanted to REARRANGE THIS ROOM!

AVOIDING 'SACRED SITES'

There's the church we were MARRIED IN!

CREATING YOUR OWN 'FUTURE MEMORIES'

What a BEAUTIFUL SUNSET!

REINVENTING YOURSELF

I've always wondered what I would look like as a BRUNETTE!

Actually, I feel a little guilty because I HAVE moved on and she HASN'T!

You don't GOVERN when your ex is ready to move on nor how they do so.

You can only live one person's life at a time – YOURS.

Instead of GUILT, why not feel – and demonstrate – COMPASSION?

If you HAVE moved on (and reached FORGIVENESS) you can HELP your ex move on by being KIND, RESPECTFUL and CLEAR.

If you HAVE moved on, your ex has no POWER over you. You can afford to be GENEROUS of spirit – and that means equally SHARING in the lives of your CHILDREN.

CHAPTER 6

Why Share Custody?

I'm not sure it's RIGHT to share custody! Isn't it better for the kids to just have ONE HOME?

Actually, there are many BENEFICIAL REASONS to share custody with your child's other parent.

1. It's the EASIEST TRANSITION for your kids as they will still have equal access to BOTH PARENTS just as they did when you were TOGETHER.

2. The role of each parent is UNIQUE and cannot be filled by either person. BOTH parents are essential in their children's lives.

3. Making one parent redundant in our children's lives teaches them that that GENDER isn't important and they may continue the cycle when they have their own children.

4. It gives children the opportunity to call both households their 'HOME' so they don't feel like VISITORS in either home.

5. It allows them to BOND with both families and extended families including new siblings.

6. Both parents have TIME AWAY from their children to rest, work and even socialise. In saying this, although you may not be physically present in both households, of course, you are still parenting 100% of the time.

7. Your children build RESILIENCE by learning to adapt to two different households.

8. Children are exposed to different LIFE VIEWS, TRADITIONS, CULTURES and BELIEF SYSTEMS.

9. NEW RELATIONSHIPS for the parents can bring more people to love your child.

There is STRONG EVIDENCE that children do BETTER with CO-PARENTING.

Statistics show that SINGLE PARENT families account for:

- **63% of youth suicides**
  (Source: U.S. Department of Health and Human Services, Bureau of the Census)
- **90% of all homeless and runaway children**
- **85% of all children that exhibit behavioural disorders**
  (Source: Centre for Disease Control)
- **80% of rapists motivated with displaced anger**
  (Source: Criminal Justice and Behaviour, Vol 12, p. 403-26, 1978.)
- **71% of high school dropouts**
  (Source: National Principals Association Report on the State of High Schools.)

- **75% of adolescent patients in chemical abuse centres**
  (Source: Rainbows for All God's Children.)
- **70% of juveniles in state-operated institutions**
  (Source: U.S. Dept. of Justice, Special Report, Sept 1988)
- **85% of all youths sitting in prisons**
  (Source: Fulton County Georgia jail populations, Texas Department of Corrections 1992)

*U.S. Census Bureau, 2009-2011 American Community Surveys 2012 Condition of Children in Orange County America's Families and Living Arrangements: 2012 by Jonathan Vespa and Jamie M. Lewis

Statistics are one thing, but why don't we ask OLDER KIDS how it was for THEM?

Mum didn't want to SHARE us with Dad...

...even though we really WANTED to see him!

- Only 7% of children felt their mothers wanted them to spend EQUAL amounts of time with both parents
- 85% of children wanted MORE TIME with their fathers

We knew that Dad MISSED US...

...and that he wanted us to live with HIM as well!

- Over 70% knew that their fathers wanted more time and to live EQUALLY with them and also knew that their mothers OPPOSED it

- 70% of children believed that EQUAL TIME with both parents was best and 93% that actually SPENT equal time with both parents believed it was best

So what have the STUDIES and 1 1 0 WORLDWIDE EXPERTS concluded?

SHARED PARENTING is linked to better outcomes for children of all ages across a wide range of EMOTIONAL, BEHAVIOURAL and PHYSICAL HEALTH measures.

SHARED PARENTING :
- Limits the chance of AT RISK youth
- Is preferred by CHILDREN!

*Social Science Research, US Dept. of Health and Human Services, Child's Bureau, Child Development Journal, U.S. Department of Education, U.S. Census Bureau , U.S. CDC National Principals Associations, Fulton County Georgia jail populations, Fabricius 2003, Nielsen, 2014

CHAPTER 7

Joint Custody

Some people may have MISCONCEPTIONS about joint custody...

...especially if they don't ALREADY have that arrangement!

Let's EXPLORE some of these:

I'll MISS my kids if I don't see them EVERY DAY!

I won't have the same INPUT into their UPBRINGING!

My ex will have more POWER over them!

How can I change my WORK HOURS to accommodate the kids?

In actual fact, JOINT or SHARED CUSTODY just means SHARED RESPONSIBILITY of your children.

It's the same responsibility that both parents have ALWAYS HAD; so in essence, it's the EASIEST adjustment for both parents and the children.

Here's how we devised a PLAN that worked for us...

When Dave and I first separated, our son Josh was eight months old and due to his age we initially co-parented him within one home. Dave would come over each morning at 6:30am before work and again at 6:30pm each evening to spend time with Josh. We commenced overnight stays when Josh was a one year old and then increased to 50/50 shared care when Josh was nearly two and could communicate well. We wanted what was best for our son so progressed his percentage of care in each home when we both felt he was ready. It's important to note that during this time, we never limited contact with either parent so Josh had daily access to both of us either physically or by phone.

Our 50/50 shared care arrangement operated as a 4-4 cycle around Dave's shift work. This worked well for our family because Josh was able to spend time with both parents during the school week and on weekends. It also allowed him to form loving bonds with both sides of his extended family.

One of the best strategies we incorporated into our arrangement was that we didn't focus specifically on the exact hours or minutes that each parent spent with Josh. We figured that if we didn't fight over who spent more time with our son while we were married, why choose to do that after divorcing? This also meant that if there were events on either side of his family, we ensured he was able to attend, no matter whose day it was.

We wanted to minimize the effect of our divorce on our son so we ensured that we both attended his weekend sports and school events together, eventually including our new spouses and extended families. We spoke kindly to and of each other both in and out of his presence so he never felt like he had to take sides or be placed in the middle of adult issues.

Our now adult son has said that the four days weren't too short to spend a good amount of time with each parent and not too long to miss the other parent too much. He also enjoyed spending family time with both parents and extended family. Our custody arrangement allowed him to feel equally as comfortable in each house and he still considers both residences to be his home.

The key ingredient of our joint custody arrangement was that we had realistic expectations of both our son and ourselves so we were able to face obstacles and challenges in a more proactive way. This has allowed both of us to focus on what was truly best for our son.

Our arrangement is just ONE EXAMPLE of how to structure joint custody but you can tailor your own to suit your SPECIFIC NEEDS.

For example, you might like to TRY:

WEEK ABOUT

JANUARY

Sun	Mon	Tue	Wed	Thur	Fri	Sat
		1	2	3	4	5
6	7 $_{3PM}$	8	9	10	11	12
13	14 $_{3PM}$	15	16	17	18	19
20	21	22	23	24	25	26
27	28 $_{3PM}$	29	30	31		

■ Jane   ■ Joe

3-3-4-4 ROTATING

MARCH

Wed	Thurs	Fri	Sat	Sun	Mon	Tue
	1	2	3	4	5	6
7	8	9	10	11	12	13
14	15	16	17	18	19	20
21	22	23	24	25	26	27
28	29	30	31			

■ Jane   ■ Joe

2-2-5-5 ROTATING

JUNE						
Sun	Mon	Tue	Wed	Thur	Fri	Sat
				1	2	3
4	5	6	7	8	9	10
11	12	13	14	15	16	17
18	19	20	21	22	23	24
25	26	27	28	29	30	

■ Jane ■ Joe

What about SPECIAL OCCASIONS?

For any custody arrangement to work, it needs to be fair to both the PARENTS and the CHILDREN. This means sharing special events like BIRTHDAYS, EASTER, CHRISTMAS and HOLIDAY TIME.

Sharing the actual days EQUALLY will allow your children to spend time on these special occasions with BOTH PARENTS.

For example, if the occasion falls on a school day, one parent may wake up with them and celebrate with BREAKFAST while the other may pick them up from school and celebrate with DINNER.

You could ALTERNATE this each year, so your children get to experience this time in BOTH HOMES.

School holidays are DIFFICULT because I have to WORK!

Ideally, any holiday time will involve the children spending equal time with BOTH parents but this may not be PRACTICAL.

Again, putting the CHILD'S NEEDS first may mean that the child stays with the parent who isn't working, rather than spending the holidays in CARE.

My ex wants to take the kids on an OVERSEAS TRIP. They'll be away for WEEKS!

Isn't it great that your children get to have such a WONDERFUL EXPERIENCE?

Can you FOCUS on that?

CHAPTER 8

What If My Ex Won't Co-Parent?

I'm sorry — it all sounds great for YOU but we just can't discuss ANYTHING without it becoming a FULL-SCALE WAR!

Not every family will be in a position to co-parent in the same way.

For families that operate under a high level of CONFLICT where communication is VOLATILE or even DANGEROUS, there is a SAFER and HEALTHIER alternative - PARALLEL PARENTING.

With PARALLEL PARENTING both parents still have ACCESS to the children and are involved in DECISION-MAKING but COMMUNICATION is handled by:

- A THIRD PARTY
- EMAIL
- LETTER
- TEXT
- APPS

The third party can be a FAMILY MEMBER, FRIEND or in some countries, even a COURT-APPOINTED REPRESENTATIVE.

Whilst PARALLEL PARENTING creates the opportunity for you to separate your lives from each other, it has its disadvantages in that there are:

- **SEPARATE RULES AND EXPECTATIONS FOR YOUR CHILDREN IN EACH HOME**
- **NEITHER PARENT HAS AN OPPORTUNITY TO INFLUENCE THE OTHER**
- **INCIDENTS INVOLVING YOUR CHILDREN THAT OCCUR IN EACH HOME ARE NOT NECESSARILY SHARED OR MUTUALLY RESOLVED**

You will still need to come to agreement about GUARDIANSHIP ISSUES such as:

EDUCATION   RELIGION   MEDICAL

People will argue that they can't CO-PARENT because…

1. My ex LEFT ME and THE KIDS when he had his affair!

2. My ex is a COMPLETE NARCISSIST!

3. My ex doesn't pay me ENOUGH child support!

Do any of these things really prevent your ex from being a good PARENT to your child?

Let's try REFRAMING these ISSUES:

1. He could have HANDLED IT BETTER but I need to remember that he left our RELATIONSHIP, not our CHILDREN.

2. We don't have to LIKE each other to co-parent well. Her BEHAVIOUR is no longer my PROBLEM.

3. He supports our children in other ways — TIME, LOVE and DISCIPLINE — those things COUNT!

Whilst you cannot control your EX'S BEHAVIOUR, you can control your OWN towards your EX.

For your CHILDREN'S SAKE, in their presence, you can choose to...

- **NEVER CRITICISE OR PUT YOUR EX DOWN**
- **SPEAK POSITIVELY ABOUT YOUR EX**
- **LOOK FOR THE WAYS IN WHICH THEY DO SUPPORT AND CARE FOR YOUR CHILDREN**
- **BE RESPECTFUL OF YOUR EX AS A PARENT OF YOUR CHILD**
- **REMEMBER THAT YOUR CHILD IS CONNECTED TO BOTH OF YOU**

Over time, some couples are able to work through their issues and move towards a more PROACTIVE and COOPERATIVE form of traditional co-parenting.

CHAPTER 9

Formulating a Parenting Plan

Many QUESTIONS arise when you first separate and although your own needs are to be considered, the most important question is:

How can I minimise
the IMPACT
on my
children?

During this time, your children need more STABILITY than ever. They need the REASSURANCE from both parents that their needs will be met and that your love remains constant.

Though it is unlikely that your children will be completely unscathed by their parents splitting up, you can go a long way to easing this process by creating a PARENTING PLAN.

GOOD GRIEF!
Is that ABSOLUTELY
NECESSARY?

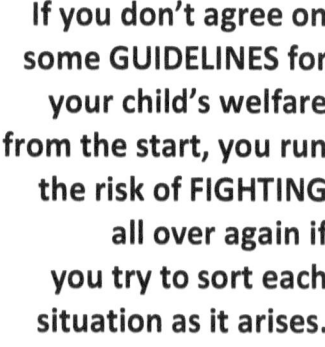

If you don't agree on some GUIDELINES for your child's welfare from the start, you run the risk of FIGHTING all over again if you try to sort each situation as it arises.

A PARENTING PLAN is simply a plan for your children's welfare that both parents put together with their children's best interests at heart.

A good PARENTING PLAN:

- Creates STRUCTURE for all parties
- Prevents ongoing DISPUTES and DISAGREEMENTS
- Caters to the child's PHYSICAL and EMOTIONAL NEEDS
- Helps children know WHEN and WHERE they are going, thus creating a sense of STABILITY
- Clarifies EXPECTATIONS
- Defines family 'RULES'

Your Parenting Plan should be WRITTEN DOWN, DATED and SIGNED by both parents. It can also be changed at any time, as long as both parents AGREE.

If you feel the need for your plan to be LEGALLY BINDING, you should obtain LEGAL ADVICE.

It's also important that a good parenting plan is FLEXIBLE...

...and ensures unlimited access to BOTH PARENTS!

This prevents your children from missing any IMPORTANT EVENTS or FAMILY TRADITIONS, no matter which parent they are with on any particular day.

The following components are important in any PARENTING PLAN:

- **CUSTODY ARRANGEMENT (include holidays/birthdays)**

- **WHO YOUR CHILD WILL SPEND TIME WITH OTHER THAN PARENTS (stepparents, grandparents, new partners)**

- **RELIGIOUS OR SPIRITUAL BELIEFS/EXPECTATIONS**

- **EDUCATION**

- **MEDICAL AND HEALTH CARE**

- **EXTRA CURRICULAR ACTIVITIES**

- **HOW YOU WILL DISCIPLINE**

- **FINANCIAL/MATERIAL PRIVILEGES (phone, computer, car)**

- SAFETY

- An agreed process to CHANGE THE PLAN or RESOLVE ANY PROBLEMS should either of the parents not be happy with the plan at a later date.

- Recognition that as your children GROW OLDER and have DIFFERENT REQUIREMENTS, the parenting plan will need to CHANGE TO REFLECT THIS.

On the next page you will find an example of a Parenting Plan

EXAMPLE OF A PARENTING PLAN

1. Both parents will have equal shared parental responsibility

2. Phone contact with other parent at least twice a day at 8am and 8pm (*unlimited)

3. Christmas and Easter, birthdays and other holiday celebrations to be shared equally on the day. Parents to have child on their own birthdays

4. Mother's Day and Father's Day to be shared partially so stepparents and grandparents can also see the kids

5. Positive reinforcement of the other parent at all times in front of child

> 6. First right of refusal to the other parent if child needs to be minded and permission needed for a third party to look after the child
>
> 7. Must not be bathed or changed by new partners or friends
>
> 8. Parents to back each other up in all decisions to form a united front
>
> Signed……………. and ………………. Date………

This plan is relatively simple because it involves 50/50 JOINT CUSTODY and allows for contact with each parent at least TWICE A DAY but is also UNLIMITED.

This gives the children the same opportunity to speak to either of their parents at any time of day as they would have had their parents stayed together.

If the children are very young, regular communication between the parents on the CHILD'S BEHALF is crucial.

It is important that you allow your child to communicate with their other parent without feeling GUILTY because:

- It establishes CONTINUITY in the relationship
- Your ex is IRREPLACEABLE in your child's life
- No-one can replace the BOND that your child has with his/her other parent
- You are MODELLING adult behaviour. If you are DECENT and RESPECTFUL towards your ex, you are teaching your child these VALUES by example
- Children see their same-sex parent as a ROLE MODEL for ADULTHOOD and ADULT RELATIONSHIPS

Making one parent REDUNDANT in your children's life can signal to them that that parent's role is UNIMPORTANT, which can affect their attitudes towards these roles in adulthood. Your behaviour towards your ex today could potentially affect many aspects of your child's FUTURE relationships with partners or their own children.

It is essential to give your kids SPACE to have a relationship with their other parent without you there, providing there is no proven abuse or neglect.

Giving your kids this freedom will enable them to form their own NATURAL BOND with their other parent rather than having to watch what they say and do in fear of hurting your feelings.

The goal should be for your children to feel secure enough with both of you to be able to EXPRESS THEMSELVES FREELY both in and outside of your presence. There is nothing worse for our children than to think that someone they love so dearly is despised by someone else they also love equally.

If you think about it logically, why would anyone ever want to rob their child of LOVE?

CHAPTER 10

The Essential Ingredients for Shared Custody

Although JOINT CUSTODY may have been on the rise for the last thirty years; historically it wasn't common.

STEREOTYPICAL attitudes traditionally saw men as BREADWINNERS and women as HOME-MAKERS and as such, women tended to be looked upon more favourably by the courts as CUSTODIAL PARENTS.

In society today, there have been many changes in PARENTAL ROLES:

BOTH PARTNERS WORKING	MEN AS CUSTODIAL PARENTS

DE FACTO PARENTS	SAME SEX PARENTS

Unfortunately, one of the lingering MISTAKES of the past has been to see children as COMMODITIES and used as COLLATERAL in ugly CUSTODY DISPUTES.

But children are NOT commodities, nor are they our PROPERTY. It is our role as parents to raise them to become RESPONSIBLE ADULTS through our own EXAMPLE. If we are to move forward we need to progress from being SELF-CENTRED to CHILD-CENTRED, where we place the needs of our CHILDREN ahead of our OWN.

Although there are many different types of custody arrangements, the ultimate goal is SHARED CUSTODY whereby both parents share equal time (PHYSICAL CUSTODY) and come to a shared agreement on schooling, religion and medical care (LEGAL CUSTODY).

But the thought of being away from my kids for even a DAY is UNBEARABLE!

But the thought of being away from my kids for even a DAY is UNBEARABLE!

Hey GUESS WHAT, Mum and Dad!
We feel the same about YOU!

And on top of this we have:

Well, I think the kids are better off with ME!

Well, I think the kids are better off with ME!

So where do you go from HERE? How do you set up a successful CUSTODY AGREEMENT?

In setting up any custody agreement there are THREE ESSENTIAL FACTORS to consider:

1.　　COMMUNICATION
2.　　SECURITY/STRUCTURE
3.　　FLEXIBILITY

Let's EXPLORE these:

1. COMMUNICATION.

COMMUNICATING WELL is one of the most important factors in any shared custody situation.

Communication is not limited to SPEAKING.
We express our feelings in many different ways, such as EYE CONTACT, GESTURES and EXPRESSIONS.

Although you may not be conveying your ANIMOSITY towards your ex in WORDS, you may be showing it in other ways such as:

ROLLING YOUR EYES	TURNING YOUR BACK	SNEERING OR NOT SMILING

And take it from us, your kids don't miss a THING!

How do you think they feel when you are THROWING DAGGERS at a parent they love?

If you're going to share custody and responsibility for your children, your communication skills need to be at their SHARPEST.

This is going to be TOUGH! COMMUNICATION has always been an issue for us!

Surely you can hold it together for the 5 MINUTES at DROP-OFF and PICK-UP time?

Use that 5 minutes WISELY!

We are our children's best TEACHERS. Learning to communicate KINDLY in every sense – not just words – is vital. Kids pick up on ICY STARES, SNIDE COMMENTS and the SILENT TREATMENT. Communicating POORLY simply teaches our children to do the SAME.

Do you have any TIPS on how to do this BETTER?

It's important to remember that communication ABOUT your children has nothing to do with why you split or who did WHAT to WHOM.

HERE ARE SOME MORE TIPS:

- Be RESPECTFUL, FACTUAL and CONCISE
- FOCUS ON YOUR CHILDREN instead of EACH OTHER

It's also helpful to ADJUST YOUR VIEW of your ex to someone who is:

- A PARENT to your CHILD, not a PARTNER to YOU

- LOVED by your CHILD, if not by YOU

- LEGALLY ENTITLED to be in your CHILD'S life

- Going to be around, LIKE IT or NOT...

...so it's a good idea to make PEACE with that and get USED TO IT!

Let's put some communication skills in ACTION. Remember that how you interact with each other impacts on how your children FEEL.

At the next PICK-UP or DROP-OFF...

INSTEAD OF THIS...

TRY THIS!

HI! HOW ARE YOU?

It may seem only a **SMALL THING** and only takes a couple of **SECONDS** but it will mean a great deal to your **CHILDREN**.

AND you'll feel **BETTER**, too!

2. STRUCTURE

In child custody, structure is essential because it provides your children and everyone else involved with a CONISTENT PLAN of how things will function.

STRUCTURE HELPS TO:
- DIMINISH CONFUSION
- PROMOTE FEELINGS OF SECURITY
- REDUCE VOLATILITY
- PROVIDE DIRECTION

Creating an environment in both homes where children feel 'AT HOME' is part of this process. You can do this by:

- Giving the child their own SPACE
- A place for their own BELONGINGS and TOYS
- Age-appropriate RESPONSIBILITIES
- Age-appropriate HOUSEHOLD CHORES

This type of structure is more likely to provide an environment where they feel GROUNDED, COMFORTABLE and SAFE.

You'll know you are on the right track if your children refer to both homes as 'HOME'. Whilst moving from house to house can be challenging, STRUCTURE helps to minimize disruption.

The organisation and transfer of children and their belongings is the responsibility of BOTH PARENTS, not the children. Children should not be involved in this discussion unless they are older (teenager).

Remember, the things your children decide to take from house to house belong to THEM and not to either household regardless of who paid for them.

On the flip side, be sure to RESPECT any items brought into your home from the other household.

3. FLEXIBILITY

Whilst STRUCTURE is important in building feelings of security, FLEXIBILITY allows for the UNEXPECTED.

FLEXIBILITY is a two-way street. If you deny your ex some WRIGGLE-ROOM, you may find him or her reluctant to allow you the same, so being FLEXIBLE is a good policy.

Being FLEXIBLE means:

- Not focussing on the exact HOURS and MINUTES spent with each PARENT
- Allowing space for a little 'OVERTIME' in play and activities just as you would have before you separated
- Making room for the children to continue the same ACTIVITIES and SOCIAL LIFE as before
- If there is an important event at their other parent's house, ENCOURAGE them to go
- If you also have an important event on the same day, SHARE THE DAY
- Allowing for CHANGED CIRCUMSTANCES such as SICKNESS, CHANGED WORK HOURS or a NEW BABY in the house which will affect custody arrangements

In this latter situation, a little KINDNESS goes a long way. Do it for your kids, if not for your ex. In doing so, you also teach your children COMPASSION.

Why should I be GENEROUS to HIM? He's never done ME any favours!

Yes, this can be the most CHALLENGING part of CO-PARENTING but do your best to put aside old HURTS and focus on creating a POSITIVE and NURTURING environment for your kids to THRIVE in.

You may not get it RIGHT– in fact; you may get it WRONG many times but keep trying! It's not how many times you FALL – it's how many times you get UP again!

Give it your BEST – for THEM.

CHAPTER 11

Child Support – Show Me the Money!

CHILD SUPPORT can create a lot of CONTROVERSY and ANGST.

I'm working myself into the GROUND keeping up with these PAYMENTS!

I'm STRUGGLING to make ends meet on this amount! It hardly seems FAIR!

Child support is affected by the amount of TIME you are allocated in your custody agreement so in some cases, parents are paying child support for children that they don't SEE.

I find that really hard to SWALLOW!

Unfortunately, the SYSTEM is not something you can CONTROL but you do have some control over your and your child's WELLBEING in NON-FINANCIAL ways

Perhaps looking at CHILD SUPPORT as not just a FINANCIAL responsibility may help both parties to see it in a different light. Your children also need both parents to support them PHYSICALLY, EMOTIONALLY and SPIRITUALLY. None of these involve MONEY.

Are there ways in which you would both be willing to facilitate the non-financial support that your children need, for the sake of their WELLBEING?

For instance, if you are a NON-CUSTODIAL PARENT, you could:

1. TAKE YOUR KIDS TO THE LIBRARY AND HELP THEM WITH HOMEWORK

2. YOU OR YOUR KIDS' GRANDPARENTS MIND THE KIDS AFTER SCHOOL TILL THEIR OTHER PARENT GETS HOME FROM WORK

3. **OFFER TO DO ODD JOBS FOR YOUR EX FOR LESS CHILD SUPPORT - THEY'LL SAVE ON HAVING TO HIRE SOMEONE**

4. **IF YOUR EX CAN'T GET TIME OFF WORK TO TAKE THE KIDS TO ACTIVITIES AND YOU CAN, OFFER TO DO SO**

5. **COACH AT YOUR KIDS' SPORTS**

AND BOTH PARENTS CAN HAVE FIRST RIGHT OF REFUSAL AS BABY-SITTERS!

CHILD SUPPORT extends to supporting the **WELLBEING** of all parties! If the parents are **STRUGGLING** the **CHILDREN** will be struggling too!

If your ex is **HAVING TROUBLE** looking after **YOUR CHILDREN**, isn't it right that you help **HIM** or **HER**?

And if you're doing okay **FINANCIALLY**, could you consider **REVIEWING** how much child support you receive?

Ideally, the percentage will be within each parent's financial capability. Putting your ex into **HARDSHIP** on **PRINCIPLE** is not benefitting your **CHILDREN**.

But I HATE handing money to my ex without having any say in how it's SPENT!

There are ways that you can both play a part in this.

The CUSTODIAL parent can:

- **KEEP RECORDS of EXPENDITURES**

This will help the non-custodial parent to understand the COSTS involved in raising children.

The NON-CUSTODIAL parent can :

- **Pay for SCHOOL FEES, CHILD CARE or EXTRA-CURRICULAR activities in return for reduced CHILD SUPPORT payments**

This will help both parents feel ACTIVELY INVOLVED in the welfare of their children.

Being CO-OPERATIVE and TRANSPARENT can help to produce a positive result for your co-parenting relationship as it may significantly reduce any ISSUES with money.

CHAPTER 12
Talking About Your Ex

One of the greatest gifts you can give your children is to never SPEAK BADLY about their other parent; either in FRONT of them or AROUND them.

The thing is, your kids see you as the MOST AMAZING PERSON ALIVE. They love you NO MATTER WHAT. You are PERFECT in their eyes, just like THEY are in YOURS! Guess what?
Your child loves their other parent like that too!

But he ran off with the NEIGHBOUR'S WIFE!

She THREW all my stuff out the WINDOW!

This is NOT your child's CONCERN. Children should NEVER be dragged into adult situations or problems; including your SEPARATION or DIVORCE. They are not EMOTIONALLY EQUIPPED to handle it.

Children should never be asked to:

- TAKE SIDES
- PASS COMMENT ON THEIR OTHER PARENT'S BEHAVIOUR
- HEAR COMPLAINTS ABOUT THEIR OTHER PARENT

as this will cause them to feel ANXIOUS and STRESSED.

Speaking POSITIVELY about your child's other parent, regardless of past hurts helps your children by:

- GIVING THEM A SENSE OF SECURITY
- REMOVING ANY GUILT ABOUT THEIR LOVE FOR THE OTHER PARENT

I find this VERY DIFFICULT to do!

Look at it THIS WAY: You are speaking to them about someone they LOVE WHOLEHEARTEDLY.

Do not make them feel BAD for doing so.

But my ex speaks badly about ME!

Basically, SO WHAT?

Why add FUEL to the FIRE?

Your aim is to MINIMISE the damage, rather than ADD to it.

Try also substituting 'Joey's Mum' or 'Jenny's Dad' rather than 'My Ex' when speaking about the child's other parent to OTHERS. This shows your children mutual respect for each other and highlights that even though YOUR relationship may have ended, THEIRS hasn't.

Acknowledge the ESSENTIAL ROLE that the other parent plays in your children's lives. Your WORDS, both to your CHILDREN and OTHERS, reflect this.

Remember that negative words about people that your children love wound THEM more than anyone else.

CHAPTER 13

Parental Alienation

Look, she's BAD NEWS! She's not getting ANYWHERE NEAR my kids!

The bottom line is that PARENTAL ALIENATION is a form of PSYCHOLOGICAL and EMOTIONAL ABUSE.

Turning your children against your ex in an attempt to INTERFERE WITH or DAMAGE their relationship with their other parent causes them LASTING HARM.

PARENTAL ALIENATION can include but is not limited to tactics such as:

- LIMITING CONTACT with the targeted parent and their extended family
- TALKING BADLY about the other parent
- Creating an IRRATIONAL FEAR of the other parent
- Making FALSE ALLEGATIONS about the other parent to the children and authorities
- Removing all EVIDENCE of the other parent from the home and BANNING all discussions or photos of them
- INSISTING that the child SIDE with one parent using THREATS or WITHHOLDING AFFECTION

- Encouraging an UNHEALTHY BOND with one parent
- INTERCEPTING CONTACT from the other parent (phone calls, letters, gifts)

The effects of PARENTAL ALIENATION are devastating for the targeted parent, their family and especially THE CHILDREN. Here is a list of the possible CONSEQUENCES for your children:

- **DEPRESSION, ANXIETY AND SUICIDAL THOUGHTS**
- **OBSESSIVE COMPULSIVE BEHAVIOUR**
- **BEHAVIOURAL DISORDERS SUCH AS OPPOSITIONAL DEFIANCE**
- **SUBSTANCE ABUSE**
- **EATING DISORDERS**
- **PHOBIAS AND FEARS OF ABANDONMENT AND REJECTION**
- **DAMAGED SEXUAL IDENTITY**
- **ANGER**
- **INABILITY TO FOCUS ON SCHOOLWORK AND BAD GRADES**
- **SOCIAL ISOLATION**
- **INABILITY TO EMPATHISE WITH OTHERS**
- **LOSS OF CONFIDENCE AND SELF ESTEEM**
- **DEVELOPMENTAL REGRESSIONS SUCH AS BED-WETTING OR SOILING**

- **CREATING AN ALTERNATE FANTASY LIFE**
- **LOSS OF IMPULSE CONTROL SUCH AS CRYING OR ANGER**
- **INSOMNIA**

But I'M the one who has been alienated! What can I DO?

1. **GETTING THE RIGHT HELP IS NOT NEGOTIABLE** Consult with legal workers, therapists and healthcare workers who specialise in PARENTAL ALIENATION. You can also:

JOIN A SUPPORT GROUP

EDUCATE YOURSELF

2. **DON'T ENGAGE WITH THE ALIENATOR**
   Instead, counteract with your own behaviour. As difficult as it may feel, always speak kindly about your ex around:

   YOUR CHILDREN

   It was NICE of your dad to take you OUT!

   AND OTHERS

   JENNY'S DAD works hard!

To NOT do so, is to ALIENATE your children from their parent as well. You do not need to DEFEND yourself to ANYONE. Just BE YOURSELF and let your RESTRAINT and KINDNESS speak in your FAVOUR.

3. **TELL YOUR CHILDREN YOU LOVE THEM** as often as you can over the PHONE, in LETTERS or TEXTS and on VISITS if possible.

4. **USE POSITIVE LANGUAGE.** This stops your children feeling GUILTY or SAD. For example:

INSTEAD OF	SAY
I MISS YOU!	I'll see you SOON!

I'm SAD I missed your ball game!   I'm SO PROUD to hear how well you played!

5. **FOLLOW ALL COURT ORDERS AND AGREEMENTS.** Do not give the alienator any opportunity to cause further CONFLICT or ATTACK your character. Be CONSISTENT and PUNCTUAL for any plans you make with your children, even if your ex ISN'T.

6. **EXERCISE PATIENCE.** This can be extremely difficult but remember your children are VICTIMS too.

Tell me what your mother did last night, or *ELSE*!

7. **SPEND TIME WITH YOUR CHILDREN.** This doesn't have to involve MONEY. You can:

GO FOR A WALK **GO FISHING** **PLAY A GAME**

8. **NEVER GIVE UP HOPE ON SEEING YOUR CHILDREN!**
   Even if contact with them has been compromised, you can show them how much you tried to REACH OUT to them.

KEEP A JOURNAL of all the times you tried to contact them or thought about them. Remember not to use language which puts their other parent DOWN.

Sadly, your CHILDREN are the ones that will be most affected by PARENTAL ALIENATION but if you take care not to place them in the middle of your issues, they have a better chance of RECOVERY.

If you are ever concerned about the SAFETY of your children, be sure to contact the AUTHORITIES.

CHAPTER 14

Letting Go of Control

It is now time to address some particular CHALLENGES that involve RELINQUISHING CONTROL.

LOSING CONTROL over what happens while your child is with their other parent may be one of the biggest challenges you face; particularly if you have a small percentage of custody. It is however something you need to ACCEPT or at least find a way to MANAGE.

1. DIFFERENT HOUSE RULES

My ex ALLOWS the kids to do things when he has them that I would NEVER ALLOW!

Some things may not have made it into the PARENTING PLAN – either because they have not yet ARISEN or because both parties have not AGREED upon them.

Some of these may include:

- Access to VIDEO GAMES or MOVIES
- Having DESSERT every night
- Risky activities like ROCK CLIMBING or MOTORBIKE RIDING
- The degree of PARENTAL SUPERVISION you would prefer
- Attending CERTAIN EVENTS (religious, political, musical etc.)

If I'm not HAPPY with something, what can I DO?

Is it something you can LIVE WITH?

Then LET IT GO. Is it worth possible CONFLICT?

Is it EXTREMELY IMPORTANT to you?

If so, you will need to RAISE the issue for DISCUSSION

Keep in mind though that anything that arises that you don't agree with should be addressed with the OTHER PARENT but NOT WITH or AROUND your CHILDREN.

It's unfair to try and ENFORCE your rules or PUNISH your kids for not abiding by them while they are in their other home.

This can make your children feel GUILTY and ANXIOUS for something that is completely out of their CONTROL.

It also shows the children that you do not ENDORSE the AUTHORITY of their other parent in their own home, which creates CONFUSION for children and COMPETITION between ex-partners.

There will need to be GIVE and TAKE.

2. NOT SEEING YOUR CHILDREN EVERY DAY

Getting used to not seeing your child every day will be particularly challenging initially but with time you will learn to adjust to your new situation.

This does not mean that you won't miss your children but you will eventually be able to MAKE PEACE with your circumstances.

Keeping yourself BUSY and enhancing your life with ACTIVITIES and INTERESTS will allow you to focus less on missing your children. It will also enable you to have more to SHARE with them when you see them next.

3. YOUR EX-PARTNER'S ASSOCIATES

Whomever your ex is DATING or ASSOCIATING with is out of your control. You have no choice but to TRUST that their other parent has your children's WELFARE at heart.

This really FRIGHTENS me!
What can I DO?

- Keep the LINES OF COMMUNICATION open with your children
- Ensure that they are HAPPY, HEALTHY and SAFE by being OBSERVANT to any BEHAVIOURAL CHANGES
- Don't ask your children to relay PERSONAL INFORMATION or SPEAK BADLY of their other parent
- Be careful not to PROMPT or LEAD them – just ensure that they are SAFE
- If you are genuinely CONCERNED, you should by all means take appropriate ACTION and contact the AUTHORITIES

4. GUILT

I feel like I've let my kids DOWN!

You may feel like you ABANDONED your children or that they will SUFFER in some way because of the decision that you have made.

You may now have more children that are with you ALL the time whilst your other children continue to come and go from HOUSE to HOUSE.

Guilt is a NO-WIN emotion. It changes NOTHING and only keeps you tied to the PAST.

Give yourself a BREAK. The decisions you made were what you thought were BEST for your children AT THE TIME with the KNOWLEDGE YOU HAD.

CHAPTER 15

Dating for Single Parents

You're over the WORST and you're now ready to start seeing other people and perhaps finding LOVE again – possibly after many years of being with ONE PERSON.

I'm sooo out of PRACTICE!

I'm worried that I won't MEET ANYONE!

The upside of the soaring DIVORCE rate means that there are many separated people out there feeling EXACTLY the SAME!

But I'm not choosing just for *ME* anymore!

There are challenges when dating if you have children; particularly if you don't have a lot of support, but with the right MINDSET, it's not out of reach.

Whilst it's not necessary to look for another PARENT for your children, it is important to choose someone who displays qualities that are APPROPRIATE for your children to be around. If the person you're dating doesn't understand the IMPORTANCE of your children to you; that should be your first RED FLAG!

WHAT YOUR NEW PARTNER NEEDS TO UNDERSTAND:

- Things will be out of their CONTROL
- They'll need to be FLEXIBLE and STABLE
- SPONTANEITY will be difficult to find
- You'll be spending time with your EX

THINGS FOR YOU TO REMEMBER:

- Don't KID YOURSELF or PRETEND that your children aren't going to play a MAJOR PART in your relationship.
  They WILL.

- **You were a PARENT when your new partner met you and a PARENT is what you will remain**
- **The person you are with is ATTRACTED to WHO YOU ARE. Part of WHO YOU ARE is your children**
- **The RIGHT PERSON will accept you AND your children AS YOU (and they) ARE**
- **Children ADD to our lives in more ways than we could imagine. Your new partner can SHARE in this gift**

I'm not sure WHEN I should introduce him to the kids — or even HOW to do that!

The SHORT ANSWER to this is:

DON'T RUSH IT!

Introducing your children to a person who has not yet established themselves in your life can be a case of TOO MUCH, TOO SOON for all parties.

For the CHILDREN this may mean:

- CONFUSION around the role that the person will play in their lives and their expectations of them
- Feeling THREATENED because more of the time you spend with them is now spent with the new person
- UNSETTLED EMOTIONS that this person you are now with is not their other parent

And for the new PARTNER, rushing into a relationship with your children may mean:

- Not having time to FIND their FEET in a family dynamic – especially if they don't have children
- The PRESSURE of PARENTAL EXPECTATIONS
- An expectation of COMMITMENT to the relationship which is not yet fully established

So how will I know when it IS the right time?

Before introducing, you should ensure that your new partner is ready to make A LONG-TERM COMMITMENT to your relationship. You want to avoid exposing your children to MULTIPLE BREAK-UPS if you can. You can ease into this by:

- Introducing your new partner as a FRIEND
- Having your partner spend time with ALL of you, to allow the relationships to develop NATURALLY
- Allowing TIME for not only your children but also your partner to ADJUST
- Not expecting immediate BONDING between your children and your partner. This will need to develop ORGANICALLY and find its own LEVEL
- Once you feel all parties are READY, tell your children that you are now in a RELATIONSHIP

Whilst your children's wellbeing is the main consideration, it's also ESSENTIAL to give the person you are dating some time to adjust to a different lifestyle; as taking on someone else's child or children has UNIQUE CHALLENGES to being a birth parent.

These may include:

- A lack of SPONTANEITY in your relationship
- FINANCIAL CONSTRAINTS
- TIME CONSTRAINTS
- CONFUSION over roles as partner and/or parent
- Feelings of being EXCLUDED in favour of the children's needs
- Feeling THREATENED by your relationship with your child's other parent
- Not feeling the same level of UNCONDITIONAL LOVE that you feel for your children

The person you bring into the lives of your children will need to be EMOTIONALLY MATURE enough to take on this challenging role.

For now, just make sure you allow enough TIME for everyone to ADJUST before you leap into the next step of the relationship.

The
Final Word

The decision to share custody will involve both parents putting aside their own differences and placing the needs of their CHILDREN ahead of their OWN.

This will involve a lot of HARD WORK, RESTRAINT, SELFLESSNESS and, most importantly, LOVE for your children.

It will take CONSISTENCY, FLEXIBILITY, COMMUNICATION and a positive approach, REGARDLESS of your feelings for one another.

There may be many times when you will want to throw in the towel. When you feel like giving up, remember the reasons why sharing custody is so important for your KIDS.

Sharing custody has many challenges but the irrefutable fact remains that it is in the BEST INTEREST OF YOUR CHILDREN to have access to both parents where each party is fit, willing and able and there also is no proven addiction or abuse.

Consider it a **WORK IN PROGRESS**, where each parent has the opportunity to **LEARN** and **GROW**. Don't be discouraged by any setbacks.
Your greatest growth often comes from the most challenging situations.

Set yourself free from your **PAST** issues to make room for a bright new **FUTURE**.

You and your children are **WORTH IT**.

ACKNOWLEDGEMENTS

Tracey

To God. For giving me the grace to forgive, the desire to co-parent and the courage to step into the unknown. Nothing is impossible with You.

To our amazing son, Josh. Thank you for allowing us to share your story and for being so accepting of the life we chose for you. I hope you always remember your childhood being filled with love in both homes. I love you bud.

To Dave. Our co-parenting journey has been filled with challenges but none that we haven't managed to overcome with a *little* give and take, (alright, a LOT of give and take). Thank you for being such an amazing dad to Josh and for always putting his needs first.

To my husband, Scott. You have been the most amazing support to me in this co-parenting journey. Thank you for knowing when to step back and when to step in. You are a gift to our whole family. Josh and I love you so much.

To Dani. I bet you never thought you'd grow up, get married and have your very own ex-wife? You have made our co-parenting journey so much easier and I want to thank you for the love you have shared with Josh. I know he loves you just as much (despite what Milana tells you) ☺

To Milana and Valentina. Thank you for sharing your big brother with me and for all of our special playdates. You are my two precious princesses and I love you so much!

To Tahlia. Thanks for being an amazing sister to Josh and a beautiful step daughter to me. Thank you for the hundreds of hours of massages that your brother has requested of you too!

To my family. Thank you for being there for me and providing sleep when I needed it, healing when I lost my way and love unconditionally.

To my Uncle Bruce. 35 years ago, you taught me how to love unconditionally through your relationship with Aunty Pauline after you divorced. You put your kids' needs ahead of everything else and now, through this book, your legacy lives on.

To Karen. Your ears must still be aching from my endless phone calls! Thank you for your patience, love and understanding. I could not have survived those early days without you.

To Monique. Thank you for listening for hours on end to my ramblings throughout this journey. Your friendship and support has meant more to me than you will ever know.

To Rosilda, Gary, Giorgio and Linetta. Thank you so much for accepting Josh into your hearts and families. It just goes to show that biology has nothing to do with love.

Daniella

To Heather, for your continuous support and guidance and for giving me the tools to navigate through difficult situations.

To Suz, for always being happy to help, guide, support and answer all of my numerous questions! Thank you.

To Linetta for your creative insight and for constantly rescuing us technologically and spending so much of your own time helping us.

To the Rigon family, for accepting me into your family as Josh's step- mother and always supporting my relationship with him and Dave.

To my family and friends for accepting Josh into your lives and your hearts from the moment you met him.

To Trace for your love, friendship and support throughout this journey and most of all, for sharing Josh with me and encouraging me to be actively involved in every part of his life.

To my mum and dad, for being a constant source of support. You are always ready to step up and help and nothing is ever a burden. I love you so much.

To my beautiful children, for being the absolute lights of my life and my reason for being. I love you infinity times infinity.

To my amazing husband Dave for your love, patience, guidance, understanding, consideration and for always including me in every part of Josh's life. I love you with all of my heart.

Finally, to the young man at the centre of this book, Josh. Thank you for accepting me as one of your parents and for inviting me to be such a big part of your life. You have always treated me with so much love and respect and I am so blessed and honoured to be your step mum. I love you so very much.

www.ingramcontent.com/pod-product-compliance
Lightning Source LLC
Chambersburg PA
CBHW021112080526
44587CB00010B/485